What's your fantasy death?

(describe it in one sentence)

*A Fantasy Death card handed out to all audience members at the start of the show, along with a pen and a fresh cup of coffee.*

**Other Titles in this Series**

Ben Targét

# LORENZO

## NICK HERN BOOKS
London
www.nickhernbooks.co.uk

**A Nick Hern Book**

*LORENZO* first published in Great Britain in 2023 as a paperback original by Nick Hern Books Limited, The Glasshouse, 49a Goldhawk Road, London W12 8QP

*LORENZO* copyright © 2023 Ben Target

Ben Target has asserted his moral right to be identified as the author of this work

Cover image and all illustrations by Ben Target; Photography by Ed Moore

Designed and typeset by Nick Hern Books, London
Printed in Great Britain by Mimeo Ltd, Huntingdon, Cambridgeshire PE29 6XX

A CIP catalogue record for this book is available from the British Library

ISBN 978 1 83904 292 8

www.nickhernbooks.co.uk/environmental-policy

*For Adam, who nurtured this story.*
*For Esther and Alfie, who did the lion's share of the care.*
*For Lee, who journeyed with me to the end.*

# Contents

## Introduction

I like to think of *LORENZO* as a piece of memoir writing to be performed live. I hope you will enjoy it as such. Rather than reading this playtext as if it's just a bunch of dry instructions for how to put on a niche stage show (which tbf, it sort of is as well), I've tried to make it feel as though you've tumbled into the journals and sketchbooks I kept during the twilight of mine and Lorenzo's friendship. So, I've kept the stage directions to a bare minimum, even though the show itself featured many elements I could have expanded on in the script, such as an elegant set (featuring an exploding toilet), thoughtful lighting design (indicating chronology), discerning costume (as a reference to Lorenzo's idiosyncratic tastes) and goofy choreography (to keep things playful). There are full performance notes – and acknowledgements – after the script.

As *LORENZO* is my first piece of writing for theatre spaces, when I began, I was concerned I didn't have the skill to make the messiest and most human of situations I've yet experienced into a piece of entertainment that reflected it faithfully with heart and humour. I found inspiration in the stories of Jeanette Winterson's *Why Be Happy When You Could Be Normal?*, Patti Smith's *M Train*, Maya Angelou's *I Know Why the Caged Bird Sings* and Bruce Robinson's *Withnail and I*. These artists were my lighthouses and I returned to them over and over again, gleaning to learn how to render the deeply personal with a balanced sense of fun, irreverence, sorrow and hope. All things I hope this piece of work somehow has to declare, too, in its own way.

Lastly, this show was written to the music of Roman Tam, the godfather of Cantopop, and I strongly urge you to give his records a twirl before your day is done.

Take care,
Ben

*LORENZO* previewed at Soho Theatre, London on 3 July 2023. It was first performed at Summerhall, as part of the Edinburgh Festival Fringe, from 2–27 August 2023, where it won *The Scotsman*'s Fringe First Award. It transferred to Soho Theatre on 27 September 2023 for a three-week run.

*LORENZO* was developed at VAULT Festival, Leicester Comedy Festival, Machynlleth Comedy Festival, Tales of Whatever in Sheffield, The Bread & Roses Theatre, The Museum of Comedy, Camden Comedy Club and Angel Comedy Club.

*LORENZO* was commissioned by Soho Theatre with additional support from the Keep It Fringe Fund (with thanks to Phoebe Waller-Bridge for the generosity, you're the real deal) and the Angel Comedy Writing Bursary (with thanks to Barry Ferns for the camaraderie throughout the creative process).

*LORENZO* was made by the following good people:

| | |
|---|---|
| *Writer and Performer* | Ben Target |
| *Director* | Adam Brace |
| *Director 2.0* | Lee Griffiths |
| *Producer* | David Luff |
| | and Maddie Wilson |
| | for Soho Theatre |
| *Set Designer* | Tom Hartshorne |
| | for Morice Designs |

| | |
|---|---|
| *Lighting Designer* | Robert Wells |
| *Stage Manager* | Rose Hockaday |
| *Choreographer* | Chelsey Weisz |
| *Creative Consultant* | Letty Butler |
| *Additional Consultants* | Alex Hardy |
| | Joz Norris |
| | Lizzy Mansfield |
| | Miranda Holms |
| *PR* | Chloé Nelkin Consulting |

# LORENZO

## Eton Avenue

It's September 2020. North Wembley. Lockdown Volume Two is about to begin.

I knock on Lorenzo's front door.

All the windows are completely covered up with architectural paper.

Long rolls.
Once white.
Now stained by sunshine.
Looking more like they've been soaked in coffee.

Lorenzo opens the front door naked.

I'm surprised because the uncle I remember from my childhood wore clothing, as all good uncles should.
Bush on display, almost as feral as his front lawn.
Penis, shrivelled by the twin savageries of time and the cold.
Altogether, it looked like a Tic Tac in a haystack.

I'm here because my Cousin Esther called me.

> 'Lorenzo's had a stroke. I've been over to his place, and he wants to see you, Ben.'

I've not seen him in fifteen years. Sometimes people just drift apart.

Cousin Esther also said:

> 'When I was at his house, there were two random people there.
> They said they were NHS nurses but had no ID.

Lorenzo didn't seem to understand what was going on, he just said "I've got people staying.""

But these people had been through his rooms and piled up everything of worth:

> Bosch tools.
> Copper wiring.
> Old computers.

What had confused Lorenzo was that they'd also taken care of him:

Fed him.
> Helped him change.
> > Put him to bed at night.

But then when he was lying in bed, he could hear them upstairs, tinkering about, going through his stuff.

So, my cousin called the police.

'It's called cuckooing,' the police say.

And they can't arrest these people because Lorenzo has made the same mistake that people make with vampires:

He'd invited them in.

On the doorstep, I ask:

'Lorenzo, why are you naked?'

'I've lost my pants' he says.

'I can see that' I say, 'But don't worry, they haven't gone far.'

He'd lost them around his ankles.

His knees were shonky, so he asked me to pull them up. Now, it's not every day that I'm invited to be that close to an octogenarian's crotch, so whilst I was hoisting them up, in order to break the tension, I asked him how he was,

at which point, he did what I can only describe as – and
I wish I didn't have to –

a *really* soupy fart.

And I could tell it was soupy because there was a line of
shit across my knuckles.

Turns out he wasn't that confused after all because when
I said:

'Lorenzo, why did you do that?'

He said: 'You asked me how I am and I'm just bringing
you up to speed.'

Today is the day I move in with Uncle Lorenzo.

***

Hello!
Thank you for being here.
Grab a coffee and settle in.

I'm Ben Target.
I used to be a comedian, still am, sometimes.
This show, however, is performance art with the
occasional punchline.

Some people call me Ben Targét.
This began as a mistake a promoter made when I started
stand-up in 2009.

I didn't correct him.

Then, other promoters went a step further and started
putting an accent on the E.

I didn't correct them either.

Then, when I got my first BBC Radio 4 credit, I rushed
down to the newsagents to see my name in print and there
it was with the fucking accent on the E, and I thought:

Well, I guess I'm Ben Targét now.

Recently, I was at the Soho Theatre, watching the Edinburgh Comedy Award – Best Newcomer-winning show, an award I was nominated for, Jesus, eleven years ago.
A woman came up to me at the bar, I'd auditioned for her before and she'd become a very powerful TV booker since, because that's the sort of effect my auditions have.

She said:

> 'Ben Targét! I haven't seen you in ten years! You used to be the funniest guy! After that first show of yours, I really thought you were going to be someone…
>
> What happened to you?'

And I said:

> 'Well, I had a colossal mental breakdown. Still going though! Still making things. Sometimes, I dream of being a comedian again.'

Which is probably not the sort of thing you're supposed to say to a TV booker because it doesn't secure you any immediate work.

I began making this show with a brilliant director called Adam Brace but sadly, he died halfway through the process. Which is, to be frank: deeply unprofessional of him.

But for a show about death, I can't fault him for going grave-deep on the research.

However, if there's any point during this where you're thinking: 'I'm not enjoying this bit OR the narrative doesn't make any sense', then I want you to know, that's Adam's fault.

\*\*\*

My Uncle Lorenzo hadn't been in my thoughts for a very long time because when I'd left my family home, unable to live up to the expectations, I turned my back on my parents and the rest of the elders, which was unfair because Lorenzo had been my favourite uncle: he was irreverent but funny and kind, things I hoped had rubbed off on me.

### Eton Avenue // October 2020

Okay, Lorenzo, listen up.

Lorenzo! Can you turn the news down please.

No. Down.

Thank you.

Cousin Esther's been brilliant and made us a care schedule for the week:

| Day: | Event: |
|------|--------|
| Monday | I'm going to put the bins out. |
|  | The recycling guys come at five a.m. |
|  | So, if you hear loud noises, it's not foxes and you don't have to call me about it – especially at five a.m., when I live in the same house as you. |
| Tuesday | The palliative care team are coming from Northwick Park Hospital. |

| | |
|---|---|
| Tuesday (continued) | I didn't want to be the first to say this but, you gotta check your ass is clean.<br><br>Because you told me you found blood there the other day.<br><br>Yes, maybe it was that beetroot soup we ate but the doctor's still going to inspect you. |
| Wednesday | Good news: Omar's fixed your wheelchair, so we can go shopping together again.<br><br>Yes, you can choose the fish but not the carp again please.<br><br>I know you like it braised Cantonese style but to me it just tastes like mud. |
| Thursday | Let's have a salon day.<br>A little bit of self-love.<br>No, not like that Lorenzo.<br><br>Then a film night.<br>No, we're not watching *Ocean's Eleven* again.<br>Because you think Brad Pitt and Matt Damon are the same person.<br><br>Okay. Let's watch something from your youth then. |

| | |
|---|---|
| Thursday (continued) | James Bond?<br>Good suggestion.<br>We'll start with *Dr. No*,<br>which means we'll only<br>have another twenty-three<br>films to get through. |
| Friday | It's takeaway night.<br>Say it with me:<br>Let's. Gorge. Ourselves! |
| Saturday | I'm going to go and see<br>Eliza.<br><br>Yes, she does like you but<br>she likes me more.<br><br>No, you can't come this<br>time.<br><br>Because she found it a bit<br>weird when you invited<br>yourself to our first date.<br><br>So, I'm going to switch<br>my phone off but don't<br>worry, I've asked Omar to<br>check in on you. |
| Sunday | Cousin Esther and Alfie<br>are coming back from<br>their holiday in Cornwall<br>to be with you. |

\*\*\*

I should probably mention at this point that I actually prefer old people.
Not sexually.
Not ruling it out.

It's just that old people are no competition.

My peers make everything into a competition, robbing us of our joy, making losers out of us all.

With old people, I just know where I stand.

Recently, I went on a first date.
With a gentleman.
My age.
He called himself Handsome Graham, and he wasn't wrong.
And, I could tell this first date was going well because he invited me to an orgy.
Now, I've never wanted to go to an orgy before because it looks like a lot of admin.

This is the sort of thing that just doesn't happen to me when I'm around old people.

When I was fourteen, I went to a rich school.
Yes, I got a scholarship, but you're still allowed to hate me.

And at this rich school, they made you join the Cadet Force so that you could learn to disguise yourself as a tree and get shouted at by large men with large moustaches. The sort of thing I would happily pay for now but not the sort of thing the youth should ever be subjected to.

So, I refused to join in.

And these large men with their large moustaches said:

'Well, then, you'd better do something useful with your time.'

So, I volunteered at a care home.
I'd go from room to room serving coffee and sharing stories, much like we're doing here.

There was Mister Swatton.
He had no hips.
So, he'd attach himself to a drinks trolley and sort of waft through the corridors at speeds way beyond his control.

There was Big Desmond.
He flew Post Office planes during the Second World War.
I once asked him if he'd ever thrown a parcel at the Luftwaffe and he told me to fuck off.

Then there was Margaret, who was a hundred and one years old.
She knew more about everything than anyone I've ever met.
She also clearly fancied me.
So, in the summer, I'd mow the lawn outside her room, topless.
I'd slip photographs of me and my mates, also topless, under her pillow.

Eventually, I got fired.

But the point is: I was primed for this care lark.

***

Whilst you're here, let me show you around my family home...

Chelsea: a patchwork neighbourhood, where the ultra oppressed and ultra wealthy live alongside each other, with the occasional ultra nationalist thrown in for bad measure.

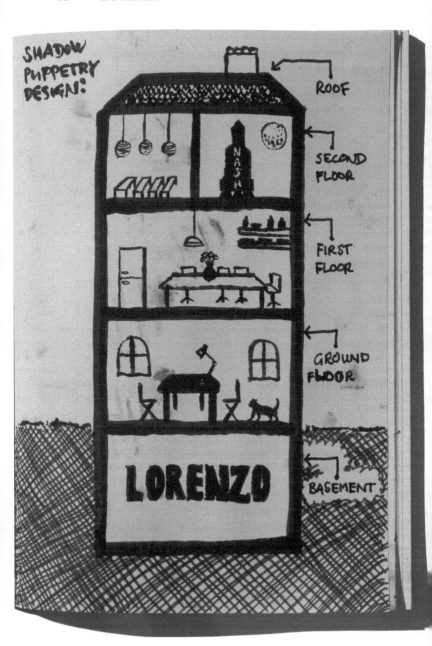

*Elevation of the family home.*

**Gilston Road**

On the *ground floor* was my grandparents' office.

They were renowned architects.

Their buildings were made from sweeping blocks of concrete.
The ones nobody really likes but still get fetishished in every museum gift shop.

On the *first floor* was our kitchen, where, every morning, we'd gather to hear the house rules:

| Number: | Rule: |
|---|---|
| 1 | Children should be seen but not heard. (Which makes the game of Hide and Seek impossible.) |
| 2 | Ask, don't get, don't ask, don't want. (Which is a riddle I still haven't solved to this day.) |

Every morning, my grandfather would plod up to the breakfast table like a big brown bear trying its hind legs for the first time.

He'd tell us the exact same joke:

'What do cannibals eat for breakfast?'

Answer:

'Baked beings!'

And then he'd turn around and waddle out of the room like he'd solved all the world's problems but behind his back, we'd all be like:

'What the actual fuck was that. Every. God. Damn. Day?!'

Which reminds me…

| Number: | Rule: |
|---------|-------|
| 3 | No swearing.<br>(But fuck that shit.) |

On the *second floor* was my Uncle Simon's Room, which he'd painted completely silver because he wanted to join NASA but then it turned out you have to do more than just paint your bedroom silver to join NASA, so it was left as paean to the family's sense of priority.

*Brother Hugo and Uncle Simon watch TV.*

And it was also here, in a long, thin room, that me, my siblings and my cousins slept in a row of camper beds. We called this room the Bowling Alley because I once rolled my smallest brother Hugo into a ball and tossed him at an expensive family heirloom.

And when the sun went down, we would crawl onto the roof and, perched there, we'd wait until our neighbour's bathroom light came on.

And then we'd whisper through the window:

'Jesus is watching you.'

I did that for twelve years, they knew who it was, which can only mean – they liked it. Perverts.

Oh, and in the *basement*, that's where Uncle Lorenzo's Room was.

Full name:
Lorenzo Wong.

A man from Hong Kong, who my grandparents had taken under their wings in his twenties, and he'd been a part of the household ever since.

As their fellow architect, he was reverent of my grandparents' legacy, but as a seasoned prankster, he was irreverent of the House Rules, making him beloved by the children.

When life upstairs was extra wild, I'd come down to the sanctuary of the basement and he'd welcome me in.

It was here that he taught me how to construct buildings to international standards, at the age of nine, which meant I had the edge over my peers when it came to constructing multistorey pillow-forts.

He would stuff my blazer pockets with delicacies from Chinatown:

White Rabbit sweets and Moon Cakes from the Autumn Feast.

And when I was home from school, he'd ask me about my day.

I'd say:

> 'Terrible! Rich Kid James came to school, and he brought his massive biscuit with him. It's called a Wagon Wheel:

> > Chocolate
> > Biscuit
> > *Marshmallow*
> > Biscuit
> > Chocolate

> And he wouldn't share it with me, even though I'd already shared my snacks with him.'

And Lorenzo would say:

> 'Forget about it. Let's make our own Wagon Wheel.'

And I'd say:

> 'Don't be silly, Lorenzo.'

And Lorenzo would then look at me very seriously and say:

> 'Ben, you could be the smartest, richest person alive but if you don't have time for silliness then I don't have time for you.'

And to prove his point, he would take a moment for invention everyday.
Highlights included:

1. Two-metre chopsticks for feeding your friends with.

And

2. My all-time favourite, the Mobinogo – The Vehicle
   That Will Not Go – a triangular car with wheels on the
   outside that can only ever turn in a circle.

We'd call this time for invention:

Silly O'Clock

An hour a day where the magical combination of
precision and idiocy were honoured.

In 2004 my grandparents died. My family couldn't afford
the tax bill, so they had to sell the house and we lost our
home.

I remember Uncle Lorenzo standing outside the back
door, brolly in hand, even though it wasn't raining.

And he said to me:

> 'Don't worry, Ben. We're still family. We just have to
> go our own ways for a little while.'

And go our own ways, we did.
Scattered to the wind.
The family left the city but the city never left my heart.

So, I moved back when I was twenty-four, even though
my parents said:

> 'Don't go. Out of all of us, you Ben, especially, won't
> survive.'

And I thought:

> 'Fuck off. I'm gonna get so minted off this stand-up
> game that I'm gonna buy the house back and this time
> no one's gonna take it away from me.'

And it is this exact attitude that led to me couch-surfing
throughout my twenties.
And thirties.
Soon-to-be forties.

*Cousin Esther visits Grandpa in hospital.*

## Eton Avenue // January 2021

There's a knock on the door.
I open it to find an NHS nurse standing there,
mask on,
holding a litre of liquid morphine.
She hands it to me.

I turn to Lorenzo and say:

'What's all this about?'

He says:

'I didn't think they were actually going to do it.'

I say:

'Do what?'

He says:

'I might have called the palliative care team and told
them I was in pain.'

I say:

'Are you in pain?'

He says:

'Not that much!'

Now, I'm not a trained medical professional, so we do the
responsible thing:

We sit around the kitchen table.

Sipping morphine from tea cups.

Trying to work out which biscuit goes best.

Turns out: ginger snaps.

Ginger snaps and morphine.
One of those magical combinations that just works.

You know what I'm saying.

Like peanut butter and jam.
Or gin and tonic.
Or vanilla ice cream and olive oil – try it when you get
home, thank me later.

After a while, Lorenzo looks at me quizzically and says:

'Ben, why don't you speak to your mother any more?'

'Well now, where to begin…
She's a kleptomaniac.
Over the years, she's stolen my passport, birth
certificate, university degree and DBS certificate.
Which means that whenever I want to do anything,
I have to ask her for permission.
At the age of thirty-five.
Also, she's partial to a right-wing conspiracy theory.
Oh, and, based on her opinions these days,
she's a White Supremacist.'

Lorenzo says:

'Well, I understand.
I mean, my mother wasn't a White Supremacist
because she was Cantonese.
But she was a drinker,
that made her cruel.
I didn't like that at all.

But if I ever got the chance,
even for a minute,
to say a proper goodbye to her,

I would take it in a second.'

### The Philosophy of Saws, according to Lorenzo Wong

Lorenzo loved carpentry so much that we ate every meal
off a woodworking table, whilst always listening to Chopin.

And it was here that Lorenzo told me about the fundamental difference between Eastern and Western carpentry. It's the direction of the flow of teeth on the saws.

In Eastern carpentry, the teeth on a saw face towards you. So when you make a cut, it is with control and precision.

Or as Lorenzo preferred to put it:

'When you give to yourself, you can best give to the world.'

In Western carpentry, the teeth of a saw face away from you. So you can get your whole body weight behind the cut, for power and speed.

Or, as Lorenzo preferred to put it:

'When you give everything of yourself to the world, you end up exhausted.'

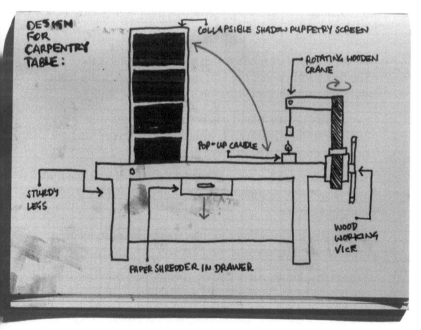

*Set design for carpentry table.*

## 跑馬地 (Happy Valley), Hong Kong

Lorenzo first arrived in London in 1963.
But he was born in Hong Kong in 1941.
In a place called Happy Valley, just above the racecourse,
where all the legal gambling went down.

The illegal gambling went down on his father's pleasure
boats off the coast of Macau.

I asked Lorenzo what sort of man his father was, and he
said:

'A bad man.'

And I said:

'How bad?'

And he said:

'He was a smuggler: Guns. People. Opium.'

And I said:

'Yeah, that's pretty bad.'

Lorenzo's mother ran her own pleasure business too.
She had a little black book of every politician, gang leader
and successful businessperson's preferred peccadillos.

Eventually the mainland triads showed up and told the
family that they had twenty-four hours to leave Hong
Kong, if they wanted to leave alive.

So, Lorenzo and his mother became stowaways in the hull
of a cargo ship, destined for Cuba, along the old
smuggling route.

And it was in Cuba that Lorenzo spent his youth, getting
bronzed and beach ready, you know what I mean.

Eventually, he was expelled by Castro, possibly for being
cheeky, or as he preferred to say, for being mistaken as a
Chinese spy.

By this time, Lorenzo's mother was too ill to travel, so she said:

> 'Go to London, find us a place, and I will follow.'

But, when he arrived and telephoned home, he found out she had died.

## Eton Avenue // February 2021

Lorenzo has asked me to cut his hair.
Rogue request.
I've never cut anyone's hair before.

He says:

> 'Just give it a shot! Use your trimmers, you know, the ones you use to sculpt your beard, to make it look like the hair that used to be on your head has now migrated to your face.'

Whilst I cut his hair, we play our favourite new game:

Fantasy Deaths.

Here's how I want to die:

I'm going to walk into a swamp
and as I'm sinking,
strike a magnificent pose.
In two hundred thousand years' time,
alien archaeologists will arrive on our planet,
scrape off the crust
and find me,
calcified in this magnificent pose.

They will look at me and say:

> 'Yes. Clearly, this was the leader of the humans.'

What about you?
What is your Fantasy Death?

The best answer will be awarded a milk chocolate digestive biscuit.

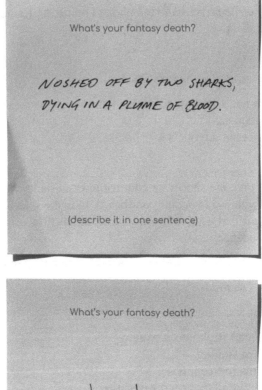

*Two Fantasy Death cards completed by audience members.*

Lorenzo says:

> 'Here's my Fantasy Death, Ben.
> Tell the rest of the family that I have died.
> Gather them around a freshly dug plot.
> But I won't have died.
> I'll be in an aeroplane with a very specific set of
> coordinates.
> And, as you're reading my eulogy,
> I will leap out of the plane,
> without a parachute,
> and just as you finish,
> I will flop out of the heavens into the grave.'

Lorenzo turns on a documentary. It's called:

Inventions of The Han Dynasty: paper making, ship rudders, ribbon dancing.

He says:

> 'We used to do ribbon dancing in my junior school
> whenever we had something worth celebrating.
> Speaking of celebrations, are you in love with Eliza
> yet?'

I say:

> 'Yes. Very much.'

He says:

> 'And how does that feel?'

I say:

> 'It feels like the worst thing in the world.
> When we're together, I'm thrilled.
> When we're apart, I'm terrified.
> I wonder why we bother to love each other at all.
> But then, it's the only thing I want to feel.

Have you ever been in love, Lorenzo?'

He says:

'No. I never had anyone.
I think it's because I didn't go to my high-school dance,
so I never learnt how to ask anyone out.'

I say:

'Forget about it – I went to my high-school dance and
no one wanted to dance with me, so I just danced on
my own.

Besides, Lorenzo, you are loved.
You are loved by Cousin Esther and me.'

'Sexually?' says Lorenzo.

'No!'

I finish cutting Lorenzo's hair.
We look at it in the mirror, and it turns out I have cut him
what can only be described as a hefty mullet.

And he fucking loves it.

He struts about saying:

'I feel like a minor Cuban gangster.'

There's a knock on the door.
It's the police.

They say:

'Is Mister Wong here?'

Lorenzo appears by my side,
morphine soaked biscuit in hand,
freshly cut eighties mullet blaring and I think:

'This is not going to end well.'

The police say:

'Mister Wong? We've had a report that you've been cuckooed.'

Mister Wong says:

'Gentlemen, that was six months ago, you're a bit late.'

The police point at me and say:

'Well, who's this then?'

Lorenzo says:

'This. Is. Ben. Targét.'

I say:

'Not now, Lorenzo.'

And he says:

'He's my nephew.'

The police look at my face.
Then they look at Lorenzo's face and say:

'Really? Mister. Wong. We were told you had no family in the country.'

And Lorenzo says:

'Family's who you choose, fellas, and I choose Mister Targét.'


### Eton Avenue // March 2021

It's Sunday morning. High five.

It's my favourite day of the week because we've agreed that I get to have a lie-in.
Omar is downstairs waking Lorenzo.
And I'm in bed with Eliza.
Nothing's happening because she's snoring like a sea otter.

And I'm trying to guess what she's dreaming about.
Is it sardines or cockles today?

There's a knock at the door. Odd. Omar never comes
upstairs?

He says:

>'Ben, I need your help!'

We find Lorenzo lying in a puddle of his own piss, shit
and blood.

I say:

>'Lorenzo, what happened?'

He says:

>'I got up at four a.m. to go to the toilet and I fell over.'

I say:

>'Why didn't you call me?'

And Lorenzo says:

>'Ben, I didn't want you to see me like this.'

Omar and I lift Lorenzo up.
Now, when you lift up an old, vulnerable person, you
need to stand behind them, put your hands under their
armpits – the least fragile point of their body – and lift
them from your knees.

Even though Lorenzo is the skinniest I've ever seen him,
he still weighs a tonne.

Omar holds him.
I carefully take Lorenzo's trousers off, his pants, socks,
easy-clean Crocs.
I put them in a bucket.
We slowly walk Lorenzo to the shower and sit him down
on the plastic stool inside.

Omar checks the water temperature on the back of his hand.
When it's good to go, Omar lathers up a soft sponge with
some unscented Sanex Body Wash and begins to clean
Lorenzo.

I take the bucket of dirty clothes upstairs and put them in
the washing machine.

I struggle with the baby lock on the Persil box, so I get
one of Lorenzo's many wood saws and I lop the top off.

Washing on: ninety degrees, seventy-five minutes.

I clean out the bucket and mop the floor with Dettol.
Three times.
Just as we've agreed.

Omar asks Lorenzo to hold on to the mobility rail.
We gently towel-dry him.

I dress him in his softest, navy-blue tracksuit and walk
him back to bed.

I make Lorenzo a fresh mug of coffee in his favourite
mug. The green and white striped one.

I make him a packet of instant noodles, the one in the red
and black packet, but this time, I leave out the chilli sauce.

I sit next to him on the bed.
I put the beautiful patchwork quilt that Cousin Esther has
made him around his shoulders.

He doesn't look at me.

He picks at his food.

He stares at the floor.

And I promise him:

This will not happen again.

## Eton Avenue // April 2021

Okay, Lorenzo, new week, new you, new care schedule from Cousin Esther.

| Day: | Event: |
|---|---|
| Monday | I'm gonna put the bins out. We've got a new one for your pads. I've written 'Stinky Bin' on the side, so good luck to the foxes with that one. |
| Tuesday | The palliative care team have given you a lot of medicine. I know you hate it.<br><br>So, I was thinking, instead of arranging it by day of the week, we could arrange it by colour, you know, like: Taste The Rainbow.<br><br>You're right, that is a bad idea. |
| Wednesday | I'll do the shopping. Any special requests? How about a Wagon Wheel?<br><br>No, you're right, it would play havoc with your stomach. |

| Wednesday (continued) | Yes, you probably would end up pissing out of your arse.<br><br>I believe that's called a Number Three. |
|---|---|
| Thursday | Cousin Esther and Alfie have ordered you a brand new toilet.<br>Apparently it's very fancy. |
| Friday | *GoldenEye*.<br>The dawning of the Brosnan era.<br>Get ready for chest hair. |

I've actually cancelled my weekend plans with Eliza.

No, she understands.

Anyway, I was thinking, maybe you and I could have some fun,
invent a new game,
bring back Silly O'Clock!

## Eton Avenue // May 2021

I'm shaving Lorenzo's face.
He has asked me to, btw.

He turns on the twenty-four-hour news channel.

I hate this.
I feel like we're being swallowed by a doom spiral.

I try to distract him. I say:

'My brother Hugo has sent us a book. It's called: *The Darwin Awards – Humanity's Stoopidest Deaths*.

Did you know that thirty-seven people have died in the United States of America by accidentally pulling a vending machine on top of themselves?
I mean, Twinkies are good but not *that* good.'

Lorenzo's not in the mood for this today.

I finish shaving him and say:

'You look smooth enough to finally hit those Cuban dance floors.'

Lorenzo doesn't laugh. Tough crowd.

Instead he says:

'Ben, what happened to Lance Armstrong?'

I'm like:

'Er, what? I think he cheated.'

Lorenzo says:

'I thought all cyclists cheated?'

I say:

'Yes, but he's the one who got caught.'

Lorenzo says:

'What a way to be remembered.'

I say:

'How do you want to be remembered, Lorenzo?'

He says:

'Oh, I won't be. I haven't done anything important with my life.'

I say:

> 'But what about all the small things, the good things,
> surely they add up?
> Grandpa always told me you were the "Details Guy".
> When you made buildings together, you did all the
> small bits that actually serve people.'

Lorenzo's not convinced.

So, the next morning, I get into full biohazard gear and
walk into the heart of London.

I photograph all the bits of the buildings that I know he's
responsible for:

☑ Brass door handles, instead of steel ones – ever so
slightly warmer to the touch in winter.

☑ Doorways, wide enough for wheelchairs to fit through,
without compromise.

☑ Rounded corners on café tables – to protect waiters
from sharp edges in the bustle.

I hand these pictures on his bedroom wall, and I say:

> 'Look, Lorenzo, your legacy!'

He says:

> 'Take them down.'

I say:

> 'But Lorenzo, this took me four hours.'

He says:

> 'But I didn't ask you to do it.'

But when his back's turned, I don't take them down,
I hang them higher up the wall.

And when my back's turned, he takes out his telescopic walking stick and knocks them down.

He says:

'Ben. Good design is invisible. And a good designer should be too.'

But I'm not hearing this.

I pick up a single picture, a detail of a toilet, I walk into his bathroom and drill it into the wall.

I look back at him. I'm trying to be irreverent but I can see I am not being funny or kind.

I say:

'I'm sorry, Lorenzo. How can I make up for it?'

He says:

'Well, since you asked. I'd like a coffee. But not just any old coffee. I want the coffee my parents used to give me when I was a child.'

I say:

'Your parents gave you coffee when you were a child?!'

Lorenzo says:

'My parents ran a highly successful, international drug-smuggling network. Giving caffeine to a six-year-old was the least of their sins.'

The coffee Lorenzo wanted is made by Maxwell House. Yes, you've heard of it, but it's not the basic stuff. This stuff came premixed, in a soda can.

I mask up and follow his directions to a Pan-Asian Supermarket on Queensway. But they don't have it in. They recommend a place in Soho. But they don't have it either. Twenty stores later, I return home, empty-handed.

I say:

'I'm sorry, Lorenzo, but I couldn't find it.'

And he says:

'I know. They discontinued it in 1971.'

One. All.

\*\*\*

*I roll out a toilet on wheels.*

\*\*\*

Great news, Lorenzo!
Your new toilet's here.
It's the Mercedes-Benz of toilets.
It's got wheels on, so it comes to you.
No more accidents.

Now that's something worth celebrating!

\*\*\*

*I perform a ribbon dance using toilet roll.*

*I lift up the toilet seat and a plume of brown confetti blasts out of the U-bend into the air.*

\*\*\*

Needless to say Lorenzo wasn't impressed.

\*\*\*

*I wheel the toilet away.*

\*\*\*

**Eton Avenue // June 2021**

Eliza comes to say goodbye.
There's a brighter future out there.
I understand.
I wish her the best.
I still do.

Cousin Esther has prepared a new care schedule, but
what's the point?
Every day's the same now…

I wake up at four a.m.
Fumble my way downstairs.

I lift Lorenzo's fluid-heavy legs out of bed.
Walk him to the bathroom.
He leaks from new places.
I mop up the splashes.

He turns films off halfway through.

He says:

    'I can't concentrate.'

He stops listening to me when I read aloud from his
favourite magazine, *The New Scientist*.

He says:

    'What's the point?'

Even though we have to eat the same dishes every day.
He still criticises my cooking.

He says he doesn't want me here.
But I tell him he can't be alone.

He pisses in cups.
Bowls.
Plant pots.
Anything vaguely cylindrical.

I once find him pissing into the mesh of his expensive office chair.
It fans out and cascades across the floor.

It looks fun.

It isn't fun.

He still resents me seeing him like this.
And I resent him for resenting me.

He becomes mean.
I get snide.

We stop talking.

I still show up for what's needed.
But mentally, I've checked out.

There is no dignity.

I know you already know this, but it's just shit watching someone you love die, when there's nothing you can do to help.

Lorenzo and I come up with our own care routine.

To help him sleep at night, he's asked me to feed him a spoonful of morphine.
To sing him a Cantonese lullaby.
And to turn out the lights.

On the second night, he asks for two spoons of morphine.
I give it to him.
Lullaby.
Lights.

The next night, Lorenzo asks for three spoons of morphine and I think:

   'Maybe his tolerance has gone up.'

So, I give it to him.

Lullaby.
Lights.

The next night he asks for four spoons of morphine.
And I'm about to give it to him, when I think:

Hold up a sec.

I go upstairs, grab my phone and search:

> how many spoons morphine lethal?

And then I search:

> euthanasia laws UK

I go downstairs and sit on the edge of Lorenzo's bed and
I say to him:

> 'Lorenzo, if I give you four spoons of morphine, you
> will die.'

And he says:

> 'I know.'

And then I say:

> 'And if you die, I will go to prison for fourteen years.'

And he says:

> 'Yeaaah, but you're a good boy, you'd get out in three.'


## The Night of Nights (New Material Night) at Camden Comedy Club // August 2021

The clubs are open again and I return to my first love:
stand-up.

***

> 'Okay, I'm gonna do an impression. All I need from
> you guys is complete silence.'

\*\*\*

*I crab-walk across the stage.*
*When I reach the other side, I take my hat off and place it*
*on the ground.*
*I crab-walk back across the stage.*

\*\*\*

'Hermit crab moves to the big city. Downsizes.
Can't afford the rent. Has to leave.'

Needless to say, that audience wasn't impressed.

I walk home at one a.m. and see Lorenzo's bedroom light
is on. Odd. Because he goes to sleep at seven-thirty p.m.
I open the door slowly, expecting to find a disaster but
Lorenzo is sitting up in his armchair.

I say:

'What's going on?'

Lorenzo says:

'Ben! My toenails are too long, and you know I can't
sleep with long toenails.'

I say:

'Fine, I'll fetch the angle grinder then.'

So, I'm sanding Lorenzo's talons.

And he asks me:

'How was your gig?'

I say:

'Fucking dreadful. The audience absolutely hated me.'

Lorenzo says:

'What, all of them?'

I say:

> 'Well, no, two of them came up to me at the end and told me how much they appreciated what I was trying to do.'

Lorenzo says:

> 'Two is good.'

And I say:

> 'Not if you wanna pay the bills.'

Lorenzo says:

> 'Oh, is that why you do it then?'

I say:

> 'I don't know any more. When I started, I thought if I got famous my parents would finally respect me. But they didn't even come to see me at my best, eleven years ago, when I got that nomination. So, that was stupid. Still, sometimes, I think about making a comeback.'

Lorenzo says:

> 'Yeah, but, technically, in order to make an actual comeback, you'd have to be famous first.'

**Eton Avenue // November 2021**

I'm offered an interview at a rich school.
Ideal.
Three days a week.
And a salary.
My own studio.

The parents here don't care about art, so there's no pressure to be a good teacher.

And, my god, the facilities are lush.
I could picture myself here, making cute Etsy postcards
on the side.
And for the first time in what feels like forever, I'm
excited.

I wake up early to prepare for the interview and find two
things have happened:

1. Lorenzo has shat the bed.

And

2. Somehow, my mother has stolen my DBS certificate.
   Again.

I deal with number one first:

I'm on my own now.
But even so, I lift Lorenzo out of bed.
I hold him up with one hand, strip his clothes off with the
other.
Into the shower.
I tell him I'm in a rush, so I give him the sponge.
But he just stares at it.
I try to wash him carefully.
He complains I'm being rough.

Back to bed.
Fresh mug of coffee, just the way he likes it – scalding
hot.
Close to impossible for me to carry in my delicate mittens
but perfectly fine for him to hold in his gnarled asbestos
claws.
He turns the twenty-four-hour news cycle on and cranks
up the volume.

I'm on the train.
I reek of Dettol.

But for some reason, the Head of Art is impressed by me. Apparently ten years on the Fringe means something.

I walk through the corridors spaffing compliments about her students' work – probably shouldn't use the word spaffing – and I think:

This. Is. It.
Then the Head of HR runs up to me and says:

> 'Mister Targét, there's someone calling the school switchboard for you. He says his name is Mister Lorenzo Wong.'

I glance at my phone. Fifty-nine missed calls. I say:

> 'Ah. Yes. That's the old man I look after. Well, he's actually my uncle.'

The Head of HR says:

> 'Your uncle? It says at the top of your CV that you're a professional care worker.'

And I say:

> 'Well, I am, sort of. It's a long story.'

Which is probably not the sort of thing you're supposed to say to a Head of HR because it doesn't secure you any immediate work.

I rush across town. My calls are going straight to voicemail.

I open Lorenzo's bedroom door, expecting to find a disaster, but what I do find is Lorenzo sitting up in his armchair, looking cosy.

I say:

> 'Lorenzo? What's going on?'

He says:

'Ben, I was thinking maybe you could get us an aubergine for dinner.'

And I say:

'Is that it? Fifty-nine missed calls for a fucking aubergine?!'

He shrugs.
I go upstairs.
I call my brother Hugo on Zoom.

And I say:

'I don't wanna do this any more.
He's not showing me any respect.
None of you are showing me any respect.
I'm on my own here.
Where the fuck are our elders?!
I haven't seen a single one of them here, not even once.
All of them with their fancy houses, fancy cars, fancy jobs.
And what do I have to show for all of this?'

Hugo says:

'You know if we lived in London, we'd be there with you.'

I say:

'But you're not. You never are. You guys only ever come here when you want something from me: a silly little show or some fucking carpentry for your house.
He used to be different.
He used to be kind.
Lorenzo was the only one who was kind.
And now he's just the same as everyone else.'

And Hugo, to his great credit, says:

'You're doing really well. It'll be over soon.'

And I say:

'Well, I hope it is.
I don't want to be here.
He doesn't want to be here.
I wish he'd just die.
And then, when this pandemic's over,
I'm going to make something of myself.
And the next time any of you come to me for help, I'll say "No".

You know I don't mean any of this, right?
But then,
I also mean every word of it.'

I closed the laptop and walked downstairs.
And this is when I see,
I'd left Lorenzo's bedroom door open.

So, I go inside and sit down next to him at the end of his bed.

He was very quiet.

'You heard what I said, right?'

He nods.

I say:

'This is really hard and I need you to help me.'

And Lorenzo says:

'Well then, Ben, I think it's time for you to go.'

*Brother Hugo in Skye.*

I go upstairs. I pack my bags. I call Cousin Esther and
Alfie and they begin their journey back from Cornwall.
I call myself a cab. I go back downstairs.
And this is when I see Lorenzo has dressed himself. In
his outdoor clothes. No small feat. He's standing up,
supporting himself with two walking sticks, wobbling
ever so slightly.

He says:

'Ben, let's do something.'

I say:

'Do what, Lorenzo?'

He says:

'Let's go somewhere.'

I say:

'Go where?'

He says:

'Let's go home.'

I say:

'Lorenzo, you are home.'

And he says:

'No, Ben. Let's go to the place we first met.'

And I say:

'Lorenzo, I don't want to go there any more.'

But I can see he won't take no for an answer. So,
I reluctantly help Lorenzo down the garden path, lifting
his feet, one at a time, up the garden steps.

And this is when he turns to me and says:

'Ben, you're my Tenzing Norgay.'

And I say to him:

'Lorenzo, I don't think it's appropriate that someone like me should be playing Tenzing Norgay.'

And he says:

'Ben, I didn't spend thirty years working my ass off for your family not to be the principal character in this situation. I'm Sir Edmund Hillary, you are my Tenzing Norgay and these garden steps are our Everest.'

And I say:

'Fine. I'll be your Tenzing Norgay. Just so long as you never tell anyone about this.'

In the cab, Lorenzo requests a very specific tune: 'Strobe' by Deadmau5.

I say:

'What's this? I thought you were exclusively into Chopin.'

He says:

'Ben, there's a time and a place. Besides, trance is just Chopin with a backbeat.'

We drive over the Westway. Trellick Tower emerges.

He says:

'Ben, have I told you about this building?'

He has. Many times. But sometimes, you've gotta let other people have the floor.

He says:

'Trellick Tower, designed by Ernő Goldfinger. Integrity.

Built for people who had nothing.
An entire village in the sky.
Corridors wide enough for two people to stand beside
one another, holding a proper conversation but with
room enough for a third person to get easily by.
Each apartment with its own balcony, everyone with
their own slice of the London skyline.
Shops, a GP's surgery and a youth centre on the ground
floor – accessible to all.
These things are considered a waste nowadays but to
the people who'd survived the war, they were known to
be essential.'

I say:

'Did you ever meet Goldfinger?'

Lorenzo says:

'Yes. He was a humourless prick, always fussing about
his legacy. I think that's why your grandfather always
told jokes. To remind himself that being silly is also
part of doing things properly.'

I remember a silly fact.

I say:

'Did you know that Ian Fleming disliked Goldfinger's
work so much that he named James Bond's principal
villain after him?'

Lorenzo says:

'Ben, why are you telling me? I don't even like James
Bond.'

I say:

'What?! Why have we watched twenty-four Bond films
in a row then?'

Lorenzo says:

'Because I thought you liked Bond.'

We drive past the Four Seasons on Queensway, Lorenzo's favourite restaurant. And I remember the day he arrived late to a family picnic carrying a whole roast duck under each arm, cradling them like they might fly away.

We drive onto Drayton Gardens, past the postbox my parents always told me would eat me if I didn't get the top grades at school.

I didn't and it didn't.

We arrive outside the first place we met.


**Gilston Road**

And I am eighteen.
Standing on the roof with Lucinda.
Hand in hand.
Gazing across the city at the setting sun.
Promising each other that someday part of this will be ours too.
But I haven't seen her in fifteen years.
Sometimes people drift apart.

And I am twelve.
Standing in the bedroom, where my mother has found my journals.
She has read them and is now interrogating me about the passages she thinks are about her.
I stop writing and I learn to keep my feelings locked inside myself.

And I am fifteen.
I sit my parents down in the kitchen.
I tell them my brother Hugo is being relentlessly bullied at school and I can't find a way to make it stop.

And my parents say:

'Good. It'll toughen him up.'

I learn to stop trusting adults.

And I am nineteen.
It is the last night in the house.
Everything is packed up.
Everyone has left.
I am here alone.
So, I invite my friend Pete over.
He's not really my friend.
We play cricket together but there's something between us.
And we get drunk on my grandfather's wake champagne.
And in the morning, I wake up in the hallway in Pete's arms.
But we are not alone.
Through the window of the backdoor, I can see Uncle Lorenzo standing there looking at us.

He turns and leaves.

And I think:

I guess the secret's out now.

But before Pete and I can do anything, Lorenzo returns with two punnets of kebab meat. I've no idea where he's got them from because there isn't a kebab shop within fifteen minutes of the house.

He puts them down beside us and says:

'Dig in, boys. I've had big nights too.'

And when Pete leaves, I say to Lorenzo:

'Will you tell anyone?'

And Lorenzo says:

'Ben, what people do with their time is none of my business.
Just follow your fun.'

*The sunset from the roof of the family home.*

## Gilston Road // November 2021

And Lorenzo and I stand outside this place, looking up at it.

He says:

'It's just a house.'

I look around the square.

I see that there are no families here any more. Just a collection of houses as hotels, owned by faceless conglomerates. Full of unused basement swimming pools. Garages where gardens used to be. The occasional lonely oil baron, wanking in a gilded bathtub.

And Lorenzo says:

'Everything changes.'

And for the first time in what feels like forever, I smile.


## Sparsholt Road // December 2021

Cousin Esther and Alfie look after Lorenzo now. And I returned to my fussy little room in a scruffy Finsbury Park basement flat.

Lorenzo and I still texted each other.

He once texted me an emoji of an aubergine – I don't think he meant it sexually.

I texted him that I'd seen the new Bond film: spoiler alert, Bond dies.

Lorenzo texted back: About time.

I get a job in a bakery for less than Living Wage. All my colleagues are fifteen years younger than me: stronger, smarter, sexier – there is hope for the future.

And I celebrate, by going out and getting…

COVID.

But as I lie recovering, I remember something Lorenzo once said:

> That if he ever got the chance to say a proper goodbye to his mother, even for a minute, then he'd have taken it in a second.

So, I make up my mind. When I'm better, I will.


## Stroud Green Road // January 2022

Opposite the bus stop, I see a new Pan Asian supermarket has opened up. I go inside. And that's when I see it, reissued for the first time since 1971: Maxwell House coffee in a soda can.

I buy him a can, some flowers and a card.

And on the bus, I begin to write down everything I've always wanted to tell him.

And that's when my Cousin Esther calls.

She says:

> 'Lorenzo's dead.'


## Eton Avenue // January 2022

Lorenzo is lying in his room.

His mouth is open and I think:

> Should I pour the coffee in?

16 January 2022

Dear Lorenzo,

Thank you for your friendship, idiosyncracies and mischief.

For letting me spin on your expensive office chair when I was 7 years old, even though you knew it pissed my grandparents off.

For letting me practise drawing at your desk, even when you had an important deadline.

For the sweet and sour chicken, mooncakes and evenings gorging ourselves on London's finest and worst takeaways.

Mostly, I want to thank you for being the only adult I ever felt truly safe around.

I will miss you but I will find some sort of ridiculous way to celebrate you, because even though you said a good designer should be invisible, you were not invisible to me.

You will always be the family I chose.

Goodbye for now.

Love Ben

*Ben's handwritten card to Lorenzo.*

I placed the card on his body – his crotch, to be exact,
I thought it was finally time he covered up.

As I stepped out of the room, I turned and looked at him
one last time and that's when I noticed: he'd kept his
mullet.

He looked fucking magnificent, for a dead person.

*\*\*\**

And so, now, a final lullaby for Mister Lorenzo Wong,
formerly of Hong Kong and latterly of Golders Green
Crematorium.

*\*\*\**

*I sing Sandy Lam's Cantopop cover of*
*'Take My Breath Away' by Berlin*

思海中的波濤滔滔不息飛躍起
心窩中的激情終於不可關閉起
當初喜歡孤獨要愛卻害怕交出愛
你那野性眼神偏偏將戀火惹起
Take my breath away

*\*\*\**

Sing along if you know the words, apologies if you know
the language.

*\*\*\**

*I construct a small wooden crane on top of Lorenzo's*
*carpentry table.*
*I dip a marshmallow in lighter fluid and attach it to the*
*winch.*
*I lower the marshmallow onto a remembrance candle.*
*When the marshmallow is roasted, I squeeze it between*
*two chocolate digestive biscuits.*
*I take a bite.*

\*\*\*

An hour and five minutes, just to make a Wagon Wheel biscuit.

Now, that's what I like to call Silly O'Clock.

I won't get to share this with Lorenzo or Adam, but to be honest, it is covered in lighter fluid, so it wouldn't have done either of them any good.

And so, a toast to you and yours. Thanks for being here.

And if I never see you again, then I wish you the death of your choosing.

\*\*\*

*My suggestion is you now listen to 'Werewolves of London' by Warren Zevon, another dead person.*

*Lorenzo Wong in his expensive office chair, cradling a fresh mug of coffee.*

## Performance Notes

When I was thirteen, I was fortunate enough to visit the Rothko Chapel in Houston, Texas. The experience of moving through this non-denominational, inclusive space for reflection has stayed with me as one of my life's more informative moments of invited quiet. The journey there begins in an ordered garden of stillness that leads into a sparse, cave-like sanctuary, where visitors sit, back-to-back, in a circle, staring outwards at large, subdued canvases encircling the seating. What at first seemed to be the dullest field trip on record, solely concocted to rob a teenager unfairly of their weekend, soon lulled me into a place for rewarding contemplation. I can't remember what thoughts I sat with, but I do remember leaving feeling oddly at peace with myself and the world around me, which at the time, felt like a gift that only a rarer victory at *Mario Kart 64* round my friend Lucas's house could provide.

I wanted to create my own space for reflection and reconnection. This show is an attempt at that.

As an artist, I'm driven by providing audiences with carefully curated experiences that I aim to make relevant to what I feel, in my own small way, might be the spiritual requirements of the time in which I'm able to present them. After the global pandemic stripped away from the world the opportunity for us to commune under the bright lights of live performance – a scene I once knew as a network of fervent imaginations reduced to an arid desert of uncertainty and despondency – I wanted to provide an experience for an audience in which loss could be acknowledged safely.
I hoped in being able to do this, we could take stock of life and its fleeting nature, and somehow in doing that, there

might be the opportunity for a future reconnection to our passions and the blossoming of our collective delight.

Before we began our rehearsal process, Adam Brace, my director, asked me what was important to me in making a piece of work. My answer was:

- Entertainment is the engine.
- Boring an audience is a crime.
- Art must provide hope.

Off the back of this, Adam and I put together a list of aims for the show:

1. The show must foremost be a tribute to the extraordinary person that was Lorenzo Wong.

2. The show must provide the audience with a space to safely acknowledge their losses.

3. The show must provide the audience with a space to take stock of their lives.

4. In making the show, I was not to hide. I must declare openly the realities of palliative care, warts, wonders and all.

5. In making the show, I was to learn how to write a longform narrative (previously, I'd written shorter pieces of comedy, which were later woven together).

6. I was to touch, lightly, on the right-to-die concept as one of worth.

7. I wanted to perform in the gorgeous Summerhall, as part of the Edinburgh Festival Fringe,  and the show should embrace that space accordingly.

It was important to me that I kept all of this in my head every time I performed the show, so that the experience became not about me or the audience – but all of us together. Adam was particularly keen on this being a show that was not only a tribute to a singular man, but an experience of servitude and reflection for everyone involved.

*The Set*

Adam was keen there was a set, so I commissioned my friend Tom Hartshorne to build us a woodworking table, out of which a shadow puppetry screen appeared. It was raised up as I did the stories about the family home and, similarly, packed away when I did the story about Lorenzo and I taking our final car journey together. The table also had a drawer with an in-built paper shredder, which I used on Lorenzo's mother's Little Black Book and the farewell card I read to Lorenzo at the end of the show.

During the show, I built a small wooden crane. The sections of dowel, which acted as the fulcrums around which the crane operated were hand cut during the section where I speak about Lorenzo's backstory. The crane was then assembled throughout the show in the vice of the woodworking table. All the tools were stored inside the bench along with a fire-lighting kit, which was used to light a candle at the end of the show, as I sang the Cantonese lullaby, and a marshmallow was dipped in lighter fluid, attached to the crane and lowered into the flames. Audiences delighted in all these reveals coming out of the woodworking table and then being packed back inside it once the show was over.

Tom also made a toilet, which was hidden inside a dummy work cabinet. The toilet was on wheels and featured a hidden confetti cannon inside the U-bend, which meant, when I opened the lid, it would fire into the air above the audience, showering them in brown confetti. I would do this at the end of the ribbon dance, and it always brought me great joy. A true gift.

*The Lighting*

There are four main lighting states: white, blue, yellow and purple.

| Colour: | Symbolism: |
|---------|------------|
| White | The present: here, now, in this room, with you – used for asides and direct address. |
| Blue | The near past: 2020–2022, Lorenzo's final days and the last days of Ben and Lorenzo's friendship. |
| Yellow | The far past: 1941–2004, Lorenzo and Ben's childhoods and the early days of their friendship. |
| Purple | Spectacles: showbiz, baby! Romance, ribbon dancing, fire eating and fire breathing. |

The lighting design is loosely based on the Doppler Effect, which is the apparent change in frequency of a wave in relation to an observer moving relative to the wave source. The idea being, when you look at light waves retreating, they read as yellow-er. When you look at light waves approaching, they read as blue-er.

The performer moves between scenes that are set in the present (asides and spectacles), the near past (2020–2022) and the far past (1941–2004). The performer doesn't always state the date of when each scene is set, preferring the lighting to indicate, imprecisely, where in time each part of the story takes place.

When the performer talks about things that happened in the far past, the lighting state is yellow – the audience gets a sense of warmth, nostalgia even. The further back in time the performer goes, the more orange and even red the light gets. In one scene, which suggests happenings before Lorenzo's birth in 1941, the red light also indicates illicit dockside trades. When the performer talks about things that happened in the near past, the lighting state is blue – the audience gets a sense of both blue skies of hope but also life now being constantly tinged with sadness. The further forward in time the performer goes, the whiter the light gets, which also signifies the bright lights of the stage, which is where performer and audience meet to share this story.

## Making the Show

I know you already know this, but it takes a village.

This show speaks about taking care of people, and it was made by people taking care of each other.

Adam Brace was that rare, once-in-a-generation talent, who shaped so many shows, creative voices and the live-performance landscape for the better. I'm still in disbelief that after all his successes, he sought out a schmuck like me to work with, but then I'm very grateful I got the chance to work with him.

I didn't like Adam at all when I first met him. It was 2013, I was at my friends Becca Biscuit and Louise Biscuit's house party when this loud man walked in demanding all the attention. I tend to avoid loud people for reasons to do with my neurodiversity but also, back then, prior to my colossal mental breakdown, I had an ego that didn't care much for sharing attention. But then, one day, we become friends, when he thanked me out of the blue for giving some, in his words, 'credible feedback' to the comedian Ahir Shah, whose show he was working on. After that, we watched each other's shows and discussed them at length, built a bonfire that got out of control, shared many meals and too many ciders. I used to call him the Rick Rubin of Comedy (but with better hair) and the George Smiley of Theatre (but with better glasses). He liked it. And it's something I still stand by. He did have excellent glasses.

One of the main reasons Adam said he wanted to work on the show was that he had cared for his grandmother in her twilight years and was disappointed in the lack of visibility this act had. He had wanted to spotlight that, for our generation, given the ragged state of support in the United Kingdom for care for the elderly, many of us would probably end up in a care-giving role at some point in our lives. We wanted to show what that was like, and we hoped by doing that we could share that when life gets messy, it is best faced together rather than alone.

Adam, Lee, Letty and I poured our experiences of being end-of-life carers into every discussion we had about the show, and allowed it to shape the experience of the show from an audience's perspective. This led to me engaging the audience in a display of servitude as they were entering the performance space, by handing out coffee and biscuits, and having discussions with them about Fantasy Deaths.

Adam first saw potential in the show after he'd come to see me doing some stand-up at the Machynlleth Comedy Festival, but only because the other shows in my time slot had sold out. He then approached me whilst I was at the Edinburgh Festival Fringe in 2022, where I was working with Joz Norris. He said he'd adored the stories I had shared about Lorenzo and that he'd love to make a show with me. I was grateful for his compliments, but had no interest in going any further down the rabbit hole of solo performance because I was scared the pandemic had shaved away my skill and, besides, I was having too much fun working as a director. Adam then spent three months convincing me, through increasingly luxurious lunches, that I had to return to the stage and that audiences would relish hearing about my time working as a carer for the elderly, and that Lorenzo had been such an extraordinary person that he deserved a faithful tribute.

I finally agreed over onion soup at The French House in Soho, which is also where Adam taught me to eat oysters. Initially I refused because they looked like sea snot but were actually quite nice. Turns out, when Adam suggested I do something for my own good, he was right. I wrote Adam a draft for the VAULT Festival and then we began rehearsing together. I loved working with him. We'd pace about in a circle in the basement of the Soho Theatre and I'd tell him stories. When he heard one he liked, I'd write it down and then we would arrange the stories into sections, trying to find the most exciting order.

After the VAULT Festival shows, he said he was pumped for where it was all heading but at the last rehearsal we had together, he said he felt really ill, so I suggested he head home early. I never saw him again. He passed away soon afterwards. I got the call as I stepped off stage at the Machynlleth Comedy Festival, exactly a year to the day he'd first seen me talk about Lorenzo. I was numb for about two months.

This is when the generous creative powerhouse that is Lee Griffiths stepped in and, with him, the remarkable team at Soho Theatre. They rallied around the show, picked me up, held me together and kept the production on the tracks, even as we collectively grieved the loss of Adam.

When Lee and I began working on the show, we finally admitted to each other that we were exhausted by the unkindnesses of the past few years and our key word for the work became: beautiful. We strove to be unafraid to put something into the world that was simply beautiful, uncynical and yet not saccharine. Lee was extraordinarily committed to this project in a way I needed, but didn't imagine he'd turn up to provide, not because he was unable, but because to work on a show means giving everything and that's a lot to ask for. From helping him years earlier with a show at a point he was in crisis, he originally aimed to repay the favour, but in doing so, we formed a tight bond of trust in each other that gave us the determination to see it through. Lee came to every work-in-progress show, worked late into the night with me on edits, discussed every possible story angle with me, made sure I met my deadlines and drilled the script with me. Most importantly, the pastoral care he provided me with has made it possible for me to keep going. We would share lunch together once a week in Chinatown and Bar Bruno, where my family would regularly meet on Saturdays before grocery shopping on Berwick Street Market. Here we would cut loose and just chat absolute shite, irrelevant of how the work was going. This was an essential reminder to enjoy life where possible, despite hardships.

We were also fortunate to be joined by a group of brilliant consultants, to whom I would present new drafts of the script for notes, discussions and, crucially, brutal edits. Every show is always better for the brutal edits. Joz Norris noted that the love language that existed between Lorenzo and I was mischief and so I made an extensive list of every prank we pulled on each other. This reminded me of how much fun we had had, especially when I felt drenched in the exhaustive misery aspects of the experience. Miranda Holms brought her discerning eye to every line of the script and, more often than not, cut out the funniest parts, which she rightly declared were a distraction from the thrust of this story: a history of a friendship shared between, for want of a better term, an odd couple. Lizzy Mansfield, fresh off her time working on the TV show *Ted Lasso*, taught me about principal and secondary characters, helping me whittle a show about large, extended families intersecting over decades into a simpler story, which gave it necessary momentum. She also taught me about three-act structures, which I used for the early drafts of the script. Letty Butler saw some of the earliest work-in-progress shows and, despite living in Sheffield, travelled to London multiple times to teach me about five-act structures, which Lee and I then wrestled the show into. She also did multiple edits on the show, especially on the flow of the chronology, making phenomenal calls of judgement as to when to place the set pieces such as the carpentry demonstration entwined with Lorenzo's backstory and the placing of our final car journey together. In doing so, she helped me blend the lighter and heavier parts of the writing together throughout.

Perhaps most importantly to me, we began a creative project alongside the show of keeping a daily communal journal, despite our physical distance, of writing to each other our deepest thoughts on all our lived experiences. This kept me brave and open to sharing parts of myself with an audience that I was scared to do. The enrichment this gave the show was a necessary step in my evolution as an artist and gives the show an earnestness in parts, which I think allows the audience to connect in a way I was not expecting. Alex Hardy came to the show when I was at a crisis point and couldn't figure out the messiness of the second half, as Lorenzo's health failed him, our friendship deteriorated, and I struggled to reconcile with the difficult relationship I have with my family's elders. She was extraordinarily patient in hearing the hardest stories I have to tell, in helping comb out details useful to the entertainment of an audience, and rooting the show's strength in robust storytelling. She was fundamental in helping me assemble the scenes in which I first visit and then revisit the family home.

My favourite part of performing the show (no offence to everyone else involved) was getting to work with Stage Manager Rose Hockaday. She was calm, grounded and brought a professionalism to this production that the rest of us jokers couldn't muster. She made sure the show hit its marks daily and held me to a high standard. I'm a slow learner and I dropped lines often, so I strived to impress her. The one time she said to me at the end of a show: 'That was a good one', meant more to me than winning the Fringe First Award, which was also lovely tbf.

Thanks are also due to the wonderfully supportive teams at Soho Theatre, Chloé Nelkin Consultancy, and Nick Hern Books, especially Matt Applewhite, editor extraordinaire, and to all the artists and audiences who showed up to support the work with kind words and good teachings, especially: Angela Yeoh, Claire Campbell, Conor Jatter, Ed Moore, Hugo Target, Isabelle Adam, James Rowland, Sarah at the London Fire School, Louise Ashcroft, Tasha Yiannikaris and Tashi Radha.

## Company Biographies

### Ben Targét (Writer)

Ben Targét (he/they) is a multi-award-winning comedian and performance artist (yawn). He is also a writer, actor and director (yes, that's too many things but it's all true). He was born in Singapore and has lived a peripatetic life in London, Voorschoten, Houston, Jakarta and Paris. In 2003, he began studying Industrial Design and Technology at Loughborough University, where he became so miserable that he started DJing. In 2005, he dropped out of his studies and got an apprenticeship at Mattel, where he designed eco-packaging for Barbie dolls (no joke). Also, despite the fact that he despises football, he coached a team that won the Jakarta Youth Soccer League. In 2008, he worked as an English-language teacher in France before returning to the United Kingdom to study medicine, but found stand-up comedy instead. In 2011, he won the national stand-up accolade, the Leicester Mercury Comedian of the Year. In 2012, his debut comedy show *Discover Ben Target* was nominated for the Edinburgh Comedy Award – Best Newcomer, toured to the Perth Institute of Contemporary Arts (Australia), BATS Theatre and The Classic (New Zealand) and was filmed as a special for the streaming service NextUp Comedy. In 2013, he had a mental breakdown and became a part-time gardener for an egregious music industry executive. In 2015, he starred in Richard Gadd's show *Waiting for Gaddot* (Soho Theatre, The Stand), which won the Amused Moose Comedy Award for Best Show. From 2015 onwards, he collaborated with Adam Riches, co-starring in his shows *Coach Coach* (Pleasance/Soho

Theatre), *The Lone Dueller* (Pleasance/Soho Theatre) and *The Beakington Town Hall Murders* (Battersea Arts Centre/Pleasance/Soho Theatre). In 2018, he wrote and performed a follow-up solo show *Splosh!* (Battersea Arts Centre/Soho Theatre). From 2019 onwards, he collaborated with Joz Norris, performing in *Joz Norris is Dead. Long Live Mr Fruit Salad.* (Soho Theatre), which won the Comedians' Choice Award for Best Show, and co-created and co-performed in *Joz Norris: Blink*, one of the *Evening Standard*'s Top 20 Must-See Comedy Shows of 2022. He has written for Joe Lycett (BBC Three) and Jamali Maddix (All 4), and co-starred in *The Dream Factory* (BBC Radio 4). As a director and dramaturg, he has worked with Kieran Hodgson (double Edinburgh Comedy Award nominee), John Hastings (Pleasance/Soho Theatre), Rob Copland (Comedians' Choice Award for Best Show Winner), Katie Pritchard (Pleasance/ITVX) and Bryony Byrne (Soho Theatre). He also teaches stand-up comedy at the Royal Central School of Speech and Drama, Soho Theatre's Young Company and Angel Comedy. If you've read this playtext then you already know what his Fantasy Death is.

**Adam Brace** (Director)

Adam Brace was a writer and directurg (a word he invented for his dual roles of directing and dramaturgy for the shows he worked on). His plays included *Stovepipe* (National Theatre) and *They Drink It In The Congo* (Almeida Theatre). He directed Hayley McGee's *Age is a Feeling* (Olivier Award nominee), Liz Kingsman's *One Woman Show* (Olivier Award nominee) and Alex Edelman's *Just for Us* (Edinburgh Comedy Award nominee). He had an unrivalled lust for life and perhaps because of this, his Fantasy Death was: swift and at the top of his game.

## Lee Griffiths (Director 2.0)

Lee Griffiths (he/him), after many years in various states of undress performing with Edinburgh Comedy Award nominees Late Night Gimp Fight, began working behind the scenes as a writer, producer and director, and more recently, his passion for discovering new voices led to working with twelve-year fringe veteran Ben Targét. He is inspired by a performer's ability to share both the beauty and ugliness of life on stage, creating work with honesty and integrity. If it's funny then he considers that a big old bonus, too. His Fantasy Death is: one that his children would be able to internet search for, without being scarred for life by the imagery – he genuinely almost died when a giant wrecking ball he was riding, whilst naked, fell out of the theatre rigging during a show.

## Maddie Wilson (Producer)

Maddie Wilson (she/her) is the Touring Producer at Soho Theatre. Prior to *LORENZO*, she worked on Hayley McGee's *Age is a Feeling*, which won the Fringe First Award in 2022 and was nominated for an Olivier Award. She has also produced tours for the legendary drag queen BenDeLaCreme. She worked as the Head of Comedy at Battersea Arts Centre. Her Fantasy Death is: to finish every book on her 'To Read' pile, approximately sixty years from now, and immediately die of relief.

## David Luff (Producer)

David Luff (he/him) is the Head of Theatre at Soho Theatre. Notable productions he produced for Soho Theatre include the world premieres of *Age is a Feeling*, written and performed by Haley McGee, *Touch* and *The One* by Vicky Jones, and new shows from Ryan Calais Cameron,

Kim Noble and Lucy McCormick. Alongside DryWrite he produced the revivals and world tours of *Fleabag* by Phoebe Waller-Bridge and its New York and West End transfers. His Fantasy Death is: aged 100, peacefully, in his sleep, surrounded by loving friends and family.

### Tom Hartshorne (Designer)

Tom Hartshorne (he/him) is a designer and maker. He has built the sets for Maddie Rice's *Pickle Jar* (*Three Weeks* Editors' Award Winner, Soho Theatre), Adam Riches' *The Beakington Town Hall Murders* (Battersea Arts Centre/Pleasance/Soho Theatre) and Stevie Martin *Vol. 1* (Pleasance/Soho Theatre). In 2013, he represented both Mexico and England at the Hapkido World Championship, which was a first for a Scotsman. He has thirteen international martial arts medals. His Fantasy Death is: to lose a lightsaber duel because he's busy relying on his physical rather than emotional strength, unlike a good Jedi.

### Robert Wells (Lighting Designer)

Robert Wells (he/him) has had a varied career in theatre over the last twenty or so years. Recent credits include designing lights and sound for *Blink* by Joz Norris and Ben Targét, *Clown Sex* by Natasha Sutton Williams, and John-Luke Roberts' *A World Just Like Our Own, But...* He's also composed music for the V&A Museum (2012's *Suite for an Unplayed Game*), turned a *Guitar Hero* guitar into a lighting controller (for Maraoke) and he's the resident technician for the Alternative Comedy Memorial Society. His Fantasy Death is: to fall off a cliff while saving an adorable kitten.

## Rose Hockaday (Stage Manager)

Rose Hockaday (she/her) is a freelance stage manager based in London. Theatre: *Jali, Spellbound: Suhani Shah, Age is a Feeling* (2022 Fringe First winner and Olivier Award nominee) and *Bedu* (Soho Theatre); *Worth* (New Earth); *Evita Too* (Sh!t Theatre); *harmony,* 天人合一; *At Broken Bridge, No Particular Order* (Ellandar); *The Ex-Boyfriend Yard Sale* (London & Toronto); *Milk & Gall, Spiderfly, Wolfie* and *The Art of Gaman* (Theatre 503); *Antigone*; *Pops*; *You Only Live Forever* and *In Tents and Purposes* (Viscera Theatre); *Timmy*; *Glitter Punch*; *How to Survive a Post-Truth Apocalypse*; *They Built It. No One Came* and *Jericho Creek* (Fledgling Theatre). Film: *Heaven Knows, Visitors, Ignite, Pomegranate, Wandering Eyes* and *Versions of Us*, as well as music videos 'Phase Me Out', 'When You're Gone' and 'Saint' for artist VÉRITÉ. Her Fantasy Death is: to be smothered by puppies.

## Letty Butler (Creative Consultant)

Letty Butler (she/her) is a writer, performer and coach. Her first non-fiction book, *The Jobbing Actor*, was published by Nick Hern Books in January 2023, and she's just finished her debut novel. Writing accolades include a Northern Writers Award and The International Fish Short Story Prize. Her work has been produced by Soho Theatre, and her short films have been shown at BAFTA, LFF, LOCO and Aesthetica Film Festivals. Her Fantasy Death: is to enjoy a huge seafood banquet with all the people she loves and to then be dunked in a barrel of honey before being lifted to the moon by bees and struck by shooting stars on course, exploding into a thousand tiny pieces.

**Chelsey Weisz** (Choreographer)

Chelsey Weisz (she/her) is a dancer, choreographer and events manager. She trained at Jason Coleman's Ministry of Dance and Deakin University and has worked for Melbourne City Youth Ballet, VAULT Festival, Pleasance Theatre Trust and Adelaide Fringe. At the time of going to print, Chelsey was away on one of her many amazing expeditions, so it is assumed her Fantasy Death is: to live forever.

Soho Theatre is London's most vibrant producer for new theatre, comedy and cabaret. We pursue creative excellence, harnessing an artistic spirit that is based in our new-writing roots, the radical ethos of the fringe and the traditions of punk culture and queer performance. We champion voices that challenge from outside of the mainstream, and sometimes from within it too. We value entertainment, accessibility and enjoy a good show. We are a registered charity and social enterprise, and our audiences are diverse in age, background and outlook.

We are mission driven and we measure our success in:

- the NEW WORK that we produce, present and facilitate

- the CREATIVE TALENT that we nurture with artists, in our participation work and with our own staff

- the DIVERSE AUDIENCES that we play to and engage

To create theatre we nurture new playwrights, we commission new work, we have our writing awards (Verity Bargate Award and Tony Craze Award), our commissioning programme: Soho Six where we collaborate with new-writing companies on a year-long co-commission with an artist to culminate in a new play, and we produce new plays. Writers including debbie tucker green, Chris Chibnall, Theresa Ikoko and Vicky Jones had early work produced at Soho. With comedy and cabaret, we identify, develop and produce exciting new talents and present some of the biggest international stars.

We work beyond Soho, taking work to and from the world's major festivals like the Edinburgh Festival Fringe. Our touring work plays across the UK and internationally with strong connections to India, Australia and the US. Our filmed comedy can be downloaded on our digital platform, seen on TV and viewed on international airlines. And we are working towards the 2024 opening of an exciting new second London venue, Soho Theatre Walthamstow. We're ambitious, entrepreneurial and collaborative, and take pride in our strong relationships with commercial partners – but the profits we make go back into supporting our work.

sohotheatre.com | @sohotheatre